C# Programming for Beginners

D0370192

Troy Dimes

Contents

Introduction

As a thank you for reading *C# Programming for Beginners*, I would like to give a free copy of *7 Little-Known C# Programming Tricks*.

To download your copy visit:
http://www.linuxtrainingacademy.com/7-tricks

Chapter 1: Creating Your First C# Program

C# is Microsoft's premier programming language and is an integral part of the Microsoft .NET framework. C# is a completely object oriented and type safe language. If you are looking forward to developing applications with Microsoft's programming technologies, C# is the best place to start. C# is currently being used for developing ASP.NET web applications, Windows forms, and WPF based desktop applications. With the advent of smart phones, C# is also used for Windows phone apps development and Android application development.

This book presents a basic overview of the core features of C# language. After reading this book you will be able to jump in to Microsoft's advanced programming technologies, such as ASP.NET, WCF, WPF, and Windows phone. The first chapter of this book explains how to install the IDE, integrated development environment, and how to create your first C# application.

Contents

- **Installing the IDE**
- **Creating and Running the First Application**

1- Installing the IDE

The best software for developing C# applications is, without any doubt, Microsoft's Visual Studio integrated environment. It contains everything it takes to build professional C# applications. However, the full edition of Visual Studio is commercial. In this book, we are going to develop C# applications without spending a cent. To do this, we are going to download a trimmed-down version of Visual Studio, which is totally free. This software has more than enough features and functionality for developing basic C# applications. Follow these steps to download the software:

- Go to the following link:
  http://www.visualstudio.com/en-us/products/visual-studio-express-vs.aspx

- Scroll down the page and find the link for "Express 2013 for Windows Desktop". Click "Download" to download the installation file. This is shown in the following figure:

Fig 1.0

- The page that appears will ask you to login with your "Windows Live ID" or a "Microsoft Account." If you don't have one, sign up on that page.

- Once you create your ID and provide details such as your full name and country, you will be presented with a couple of versions of VS 2013 Express to download. Choose the latest version for the Windows Desktop. In this example we will be downloading "Express 2013 for Windows Desktop." This is shown in following figure:

Select your Visual Studio 2013 download

Fig 1.1

- This will download the installation exe for "Visual Studio Express 2013 for Windows Desktop." The name of the download file will be "wdexpress_full.exe".

- Open the downloaded file. The installation wizard appears. Agree to license terms and privacy policy and click the "Install" button at the bottom. This is shown in the following figure.

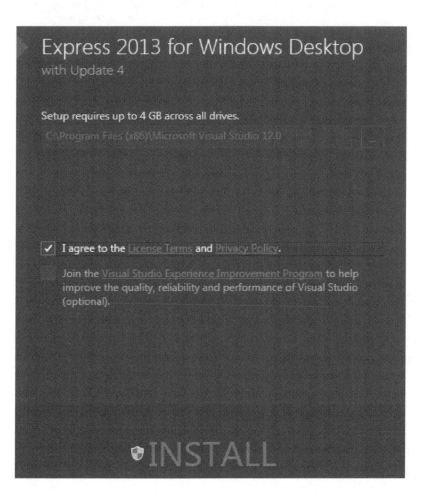

Fig 1.2

And that's it. The wizard will download the required C# components for developing web applications. You just have to keep clicking the "Next" button in the installer.

2- Creating and Running the First Application

To create your first C# application, open "Visual Studio 2013 Express," which you downloaded in the last section. Follow these steps:

- Open File => New => Project from the menu bar as shown in the following figure:

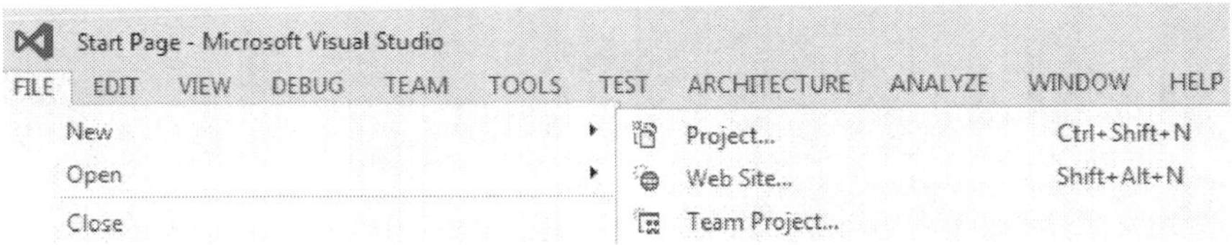

Fig 1.3

- From the options that appear, choose "Console Application." In the "Name" and "Location" text fields at the bottom, enter the name and location of your choice. Keep the "Create directory for solution" option checked and click the "OK" button as shown in the following figure:

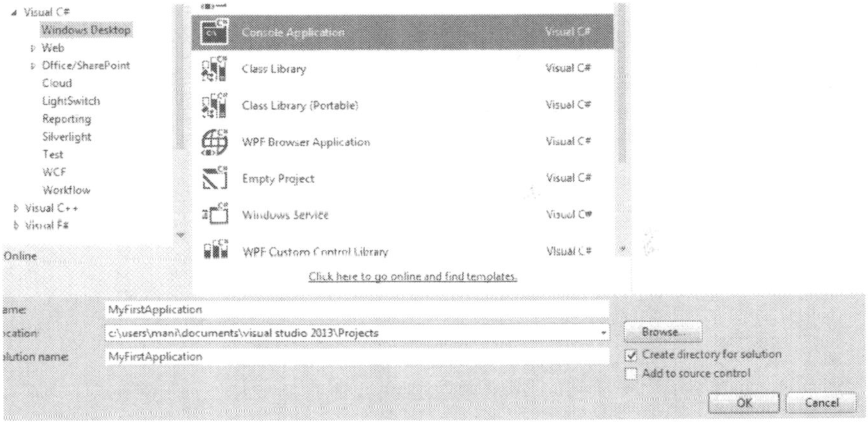

Fig 1.4

Note:

Your options might be different depending on the version of visual studio you have installed. However, remember that you have to select the "Console Application" type in any version you use.

- Once you click the "OK" button in figure 1.4, visual studio will automatically create a basic program for you. Replace the default code snippet with following:

```
using System;

namespaceMyFirstApplication
{
class Program
    {
static void Main(string[] args)
        {

Console.WriteLine("Welcome to C#");
Console.Read();

        }
    }
}
```

- Click on the "Start" button next to the green triangle in the tool bar. This is highlighted with a yellow rectangle in Fig 1.5. You will see the output of your code on the console. The string "Welcome to C#" which you wrote inside the "Console.WriteLine" method will be displayed on screen.

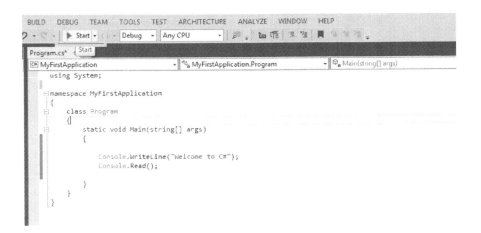

Fig 1.5

In the code in Fig 1.5, just keep in mind that everything in C# happens inside a class. The "Program" class is where code execution starts, since it contains the "Main" method. When you run a program, the "static void Main (string [] args)" method is called. The first statement which executes is the first statement inside the "Main" method. To add a new class to an existing project, simply right click the project name =>Add => Class.

You've completed the first chapter. In this chapter, you learned how to download an IDE, which is used for developing C# applications. You also developed your first C# application, which prints a string on the console screen. In the next chapter, we shall see what type of data a C# program can store and what operations can be performed on that data.

Chapter 2: Data Types and Operators

Every program needs to store some data and perform some functionality on the data. In C#, data is stored in data types, and operations are performed on the data using C# operators. In this chapter, we will take a look at some of the most commonly used data types, as well as the operators which operate on the data to help us achieve some meaningful functionality.

Contents

- **Data types in C#**
- **Operators in C#**

1- Data Types in C#

The following table demonstrates the usage of each data type along with the range of data that each data type can store.

Type	Represents	Range
bool	Boolean value	True or False
byte	8-bit unsigned integer	0 to 255
char	16-bit Unicode character	U +0000 to U +ffff
decimal	128-bit precise decimal values with 28-29 significant digits	(-7.9 x 1028 to 7.9 x 1028) / 100 to 28
double	64-bit double-precision floating point type	(+/-)5.0 x 10-324 to (+/-)1.7 x 10308
float	32-bit single-precision floating point type	-3.4 x 1038 to + 3.4 x 1038
int	32-bit signed integer type	-2,147,483,648 to 2,147,483,647
long	64-bit signed integer type	-923,372,036,854,775,808 to 9,223,372,036,854,775,807

sbyte	8-bit signed integer type	-128 to 127
short	16-bit signed integer type	-32,768 to 32,767
uint	32-bit unsigned integer type	0 to 4,294,967,295
ulong	64-bit unsigned integer type	0 to 18,446,744,073,709,551,615
ushort	16-bit unsigned integer type	0 to 65,535

Table 1.0

2- Operators in C#

In this section we are going to take a bird's eye view of three types of operators in C#: Arithmetic Operators, Relational Operators, and Logical Operators.

- **Arithmetic Operators**

Arithmetic operators in C# perform the same functionality as they do in real life. These operators are used to perform various mathematical functions in C#. Arithmetic operators can only be applied to the operands of numeric and char data types. Table 1.1 enlists these operators along with their functionalities.

Operator	What they do
+	Addition and unary plus
-	Subtraction and unary minus
*	Multiplication
/	Division
%	Modulus
++	Increment a number
+=	Increment and assign
-=	Decrement and assign
*=	Multiply and assign
/=	Divide and Assign
%=	Modulus and Assign
--	Decrement a Number

- Table 1.1

Have a look at the first example of this chapter to see some of the arithmetic operators in action.

Example1:

```
using System;

namespaceMyFirstApplication
{
class Program
    {
static void Main(string[] args)
        {

int num1 = 10;
            int num2 = 5;

            int sum = num1 + num2;
            int sub = num1 - num2;
            intmulti = num1 * num2;
            int division = num1 / num2;
            int mod = num1 % num2;

Console.WriteLine(
"Addition:"+sum+"\nSubtraction:"+sub+

     "\nMultiplication:"+multi+"\nDivision"+

     division+"\nModulus:"+mod);


Console.Read();

        }
    }
}
```

Here in Example1, we have declared two integer type variables, num1 and num2. These two variables store integers 10 and 5, respectively. Next, we have declared five integer type variables that store the sum, minus, multiplication, division, and modulus of num1 and number2. Finally, these variables have been printed on the console screen using "Console.WriteLine". The output of the code in Example1 is as follows:

Output 1:

```
Addition:15
Subtraction:5
Multiplication:50
Division: 2
Modulus:0
```

- **Relational Operators**

In C#, relational operators are used for comparing and ordering two operands. Table 1.2 enlists C# relational operators along with their functionalities.

Operators	What they do
==	Compare for equality
!=	Compare for inequality
>	Compare if operator on the left is greater
<	Compare if operator on the left is smaller
>=	Compare if operator on the left is greater or equal

	to
<=	Compare if operator on the left is smaller or equal to

Table 1.2

Example 2 demonstrates the usage of relational operators in C#.

Example2:

```
using System;

namespaceMyFirstApplication
{
class Program
    {
static void Main(string[] args)
        {

int num1 = 10;
int num2 = 20;

if (num1 == num2)
        {
Console.WriteLine("Num1 is equal to Num2");
        }

if (num1 != num2)
            {
Console.WriteLine("Num1 is not equal to Num2");
            }
if (num1 > num2)
            {
Console.WriteLine("Num1 is greater than Num2");
```

```
                    }
if (num1 < num2)
                {
Console.WriteLine("Num1 is smaller than Num2");
                }
if (num1 >= num2)
                {
Console.WriteLine("Num1 is greater than or equal to
Num2");
                }
if (num1 <= num2)
                {
Console.WriteLine("Num1 is smaller than or equal to
Num2");

                }
Console.Read();
        }
    }
}
```

In Example2, two integer type variables, num1 and num2, have been instantiated with some values; then, in order to compare them, all the relational operators have been sequentially applied to them. Do not worry if you are unable to understand the "if" statement followed by the opening and closing round brackets. We will discuss that in detail in the next chapter. The output of the code in Example2 is as follows:

Output2:

```
Num1 is not equal to Num2
Num1 is smaller than Num2
Num1 is smaller than or equal to Num2
```

1- Logical Operators

Logical operators operate only on Boolean operands. The result of logical operation is another Boolean value. Table 1.3 lists C# logical operators:

Operator	What they do?
&	Logical AND
|	Logical OR
^	XOR (Exclusive OR)
||	Short Circuit OR
&&	Short Circuit AND
!	Unary NOT
&=	AND Followed by Assignment
|=	OR Followed by Assignment
^=	XOR Followed by Assignment
==	Equal
!=	Not Equal
?:	Ternary operator used for If then else

Table 1.3

Exercise 2

Task:

Initialize three integers with random numbers. If the first integer is equal to the second integer and both the first and second integers are greater than the third integer, multiply the three. Otherwise, add the three. Display the result on console.

Solution

```
using System;

namespaceMyFirstApplication
{
class Program
    {
static void Main(string[] args)
        {
int num1 = 20;
            int num2 = 20;
            int num3 = 5;

            if( (num1 == num2) && (num1 >num3) &&
num2 > num3)
                {
                    int result = num1* num2* num3;
                    Console.WriteLine(result);
                }
            else
                {
                    int result = num1 +num2 + num3;
                    Console.WriteLine(result);
```

```
                            }

Console.Read();
            }
        }
}
```

Chapter 3: Selection Statements

Logic building lies at the core of every program. Logic building involves making decisions. In our daily lives, we make decisions based on certain criteria. For instance, if the weather is rainy, we decide not to play outside; if the weather is foggy, we drive carefully. There are hundreds of small decisions which we have to make every day. In the same way, a computer program has to make decisions during execution. Based on those decisions, a particular piece of code is executed, leaving some other piece of code unexecuted. For instance, you might want your program to take input from the user about the weather and then recommend if the user should play outside or not. In C#, this is done via selection statements (also known as control statements). In this chapter we are going to study C# selection statements.

Contents

- **If/Else Statements**
- **Switch Statements**

1- If/Else Statements

The "if" statement is used to execute a piece of code if the "test-expression" entered in the body of the statement evaluates to be true. Example1 demonstrates the usage of "if" statements.

Example1:

```
using System;

namespaceMyCSharpApplication
{
class Program
    {
static void Main(string[] args)
        {

string weather = "sunny";
if (weather == "rainy")
            {
Console.WriteLine("Don't play outside, it's rainy.");
            }
if (weather == "sunny")
            {
Console.WriteLine("You    can    play    outside,    it's
sunny.");
            }

Console.Read();
        }
    }
}
```

In Example 1, we have initialized a string type variable "weather" to "sunny". We have then used two "if" statements. The first "if" statement evaluates if the variable "weather" contains the value "rainy". This expression would return false because the variable "weather" contains the string "sunny". The control would shift to the next "if" statement, where the comparison of the variable "weather" will be made with the string "rainy". This expression will return true and the code block followed by this if statement will execute. The output of Example1 is shown as follows:

Output1:

```
You can play outside, it's sunny.
```

There is a problem with using "if" statements. If the expression in the first "if" statement returns true, the comparison with the proceeding "if" statements will still be made. This is not desirable in some cases. For instance what if we want that if "weather" is equal to "rainy", the next "if" statement which compares weather with "sunny", should not execute? In such scenarios we use "else" and "if/else" statements. Example2 demonstrates this concept.

Example2:

```
using System;

namespaceMyCSharpApplication
{
class Program
    {
static void Main(string[] args)
        {

string weather = "rainy";
if (weather == "rainy")
```

```
            {
Console.WriteLine("Don't play outside, it's rainy.");
            }
else if (weather == "sunny")
              {
Console.WriteLine("You    can    play    outside,    it's
sunny.");
              }
else
              {
Console.WriteLine("Weather   cannot   be   determined,   try
again.");
              }

Console.Read();
          }
      }
}
```

In Example2, the variable "weather" has been initialized to "rainy". Therefore, the first "if" statement would be executed. After the "if" statement, we have used an "if/else" statement to evaluate if "weather" is equal to "sunny". But since the first "if" statement is true, the condition in the "if/else" statement would not execute, unlike multiple "if" statements where the conditions in proceeding statements are also evaluated, even if the first "if" statement is true. You can use as many "if/else" blocks after the "if" statement. You can also use one "else" statement after the "if" statement if you have to make a selection between two code blocks based on one condition. The output of Example2 is as follows:

Output2:

```
Don't play outside, it's rainy.
```

2- Switch Statement

"If/else" statements are good to use if you have to make a small number of comparisons. However, in the case of a larger number of comparisons, switch statements are a better alternative. To see a "switch statement" at work, let's jump straight to the third example of this chapter.

Example3:

```csharp
using System;

namespaceMyCSharpApplication
{
class Program
    {
static void Main(string[] args)
        {

string weather = "cloudy";

switch (weather)
            {
case "rainy":
Console.WriteLine("Don't play outside, it's rainy.");
break;
case "sunny":
Console.WriteLine("You    can    play    outside.    It's
sunny.");
break;
case "cloudy":
```

```
Debug.WriteLine("Play   but   take   your   umbrella   with
you,  it's cloudy.");
break;

default:
Console.WriteLine("Weather cannot be determined");
break;
              }

Console.Read();
        }
    }
}
```

Switch statements start with a keyword "switch" followed by a pair of opening and closing round brackets. Inside these brackets, we enter the variable which we want to compare. In Example3, we initialized the variable "weather" and assigned it the string "cloudy". Inside the switch statement there are multiple case statements. Each case has a string value mentioned with it followed by a colon. Underneath every case statement, a code segment has been added. The code segment of that case will be executed based on whose value matches with the string variable "weather" mentioned in the opening and closing round brackets of the switch statement. Since the "weather" variable contains the string "cloudy", the code segment of third case statement would be executed. It is also noteworthy that after every case statement, the "break" keyword has been mentioned. This is to avoid further case comparisons, in case a "case" statement has already been matched. If none of the case matches with the variable of the switch statement, the code after the "default" statement is executed which is mentioned in the end. The output of the code in Example3 is as follows:

Output3:

```
Play but take your umbrella with you, it's cloudy.
```

Exercise 3

Task:

Initialize an integer type variable to a random value. Write a switch statement containing four cases. One of the case values should match the integer variable you initialized. In each case statement code segment, display different gifts. Display PS4 as a gift against the integer value you initialized.

Solution

```
using System;
usingSystem.Diagnostics;

namespaceMyCSharpApplication
{
class Program
    {
static void Main(string[] args)
        {

int lottery = 451876;

switch (lottery)
```

```
                {
case 467681:
Console.WriteLine("You won a mobile set.");
break;
case 451876:
Console.WriteLine("You won a PS4.");
break;
case 742167:
Debug.WriteLine("Sorry you won nothing.");
break;

case 741963:
Debug.WriteLine("You won a cinema ticket");
break;
default:
Console.WriteLine("Sorry you won nothing.");
break;
                }

Console.Read();
        }
    }
}
```

Chapter 4: Iteration Statements

While writing a program, you might want to repeatedly execute a particular piece of code. One way is to write that piece of code the number of times you want to repeatedly execute it. However, this approach is extremely unprofessional, resulting in unnecessarily verbose code. To address this problem, iteration statements were introduced. The concept of iteration statements dates back to the earliest programming languages. Their syntax may differ in different languages, but the core concept remains the same; they are meant to execute the code a number of times as specified by developer. Iteration statements are often referred as "loops" since they execute code repeatedly in the form of loops.

C# contains four types of iteration statements. In this chapter, we are going to study each of those types.

Content

- **"For" loop**

- **"While" Loop**
- **"Do While" Loop**
- **"Foreach" Loop**

1- The "For" Loop

"For" loops allow developers to write a piece of code which executes exactly the number of times as specified by the developer. This loop is perfect to use when you know the exact number of iterations you want your code to go through. For instance, if you want to print your name ten times on the screen, a "for loop" is the solution since you already know that there will be ten iterations of the code which prints your name on the screen. To see a "for loop" in action, have a look at the first example of this chapter.

Example1:

```
using System;

namespaceMyCSharpApplication
{
class Program
    {
static void Main(string[] args)
        {
for (inti = 1; i<= 10; i++)
            {
Console.WriteLine("Welcome to C#");
            }
Console.Read();
        }
    }
}
```

Pay attention to the syntax of the "for loop"; it starts with an opening round bracket. Inside the round bracket we have three expressions separated by semicolons. The first expression, "i=1", is the initialization-clause which means that loop starts with "i=1". This is evaluated only once. The second expression "i<=10" is the condition-clause, which says that the loop will keep executing until this condition returns true. After evaluating the condition-clause, the body of the loop (which is inside the curly brackets followed by the closing round bracket) executes. The last expression inside the round bracket is "i++". This is called the iteration clause; each time the body of the loop executes, this clause executes and the control again shifts to the "condition-clause". The loop keeps executing until the condition-clause returns true. In Example1, the loop starts from "i=1" and keeps executing until "i" is less than or equal to ten, with increments of 1 in each execution. This means that the loop would execute 10 times. Each time, the statement "Welcome to C#" will be printed on the console, so the output would contain "Welcome to C#" printed on screen 10 times.

Output 1:

```
Welcome to C#
Welcome to C#
Welcome to C#
Welcome to C#
Welcome to C#
Welcome to C#
Welcome to C#
Welcome to C#
Welcome to C#
Welcome to C#
```

2- "While" Loop

A "while" loop keeps executing until a certain condition becomes true. "While" loop should be used when you do not exactly know that how many times you want to execute a particular piece of code. Rather, you want your loop to execute until a specific condition becomes true or false. In Example2, we will again print "Welcome to C#" on screen ten times, but this time using "while loop".

Example2:

```
using System;

namespaceMyCSharpApplication
{
class Program
    {
static void Main(string[] args)
        {
inti = 1;
while (i<=10)
            {
Console.WriteLine("Welcome to C#");
i++;


            }
Console.Read();
        }
    }
}
```

In Example2, we can see that the "while" loop only has a condition-clause inside the round brackets. This is because the "while" loop doesn't know how many times it has to execute. All it knows is that, unless the condition-clause becomes true, it has to execute. If you write "true" in the condition-clause, the "while" loop will keep executing forever.

Output2:

```
Welcome to C#
Welcome to C#
Welcome to C#
Welcome to C#
Welcome to C#
Welcome to C#
Welcome to C#
Welcome to C#
Welcome to C#
Welcome to C#
```

3- "Do While" Loop

The "do while" loop is similar to the "while" loop in functionality. It depends only upon the condition clause. However, unlike the "while" loop, the "do while" loop executes at least once. This is because the condition clause of the "do while" loop is evaluated at the end of the code block. This way, the code block executes at least once before the condition-clause is evaluated. Example3 demonstrates this process.

Example3:

```
using System;
```

```
namespaceMyCSharpApplication
{
class Program
    {
static void Main(string[] args)
        {
inti = 1;

do
            {
Console.WriteLine("Welcome to C#");
i++;


            }
while (i<= 10) ;

Console.Read();
        }
    }
}
```

In Example3, you can see that the body of the loop starts with a keyword, "do", followed by the code block. At the end of the code block you can see the "while" keyword. The condition clause is evaluated here, but before reaching this point of code, the loop has executed at least once. The output will again display "Welcome to C#" on the console, but this time using the "do while" loop.

Output3:

```
Welcome to C#
Welcome to C#
Welcome to C#
```

```
Welcome to C#
Welcome to C#
Welcome to C#
Welcome to C#
Welcome to C#
Welcome to C#
Welcome to C#
```

4- "Foreach" Loop

In C#, the "foreach" loop iterates over all those objects which can be enumerated. Most of the .NET types which contain list or sets of elements are enumerable. For example, arrays and strings. They can be iterated using a "foreach" loop since they store collections of items. This concept has been demonstrated in Example4.

Example4:

```
using System;

namespaceMyCSharpApplication
{
class Program
    {
static void Main(string[] args)
        {

foreach (char c in "Welcome to C#")
            {
Console.WriteLine(c);


            }

Console.Read();
```

```
            }
        }
    }
```

Pay attention to the body of the "foreach" loop. It starts with a variable, which is "char c" in this case. Here, the type used for the variable is char because we are iterating over the string "Welcome to C#" and each item of this string is of the "char" type. Then we used the keyword "in". This keyword has to be used whenever you are using a "foreach" loop to iterate over a collection. Finally, we have to enter the name of the collection on which we want to enumerate. The "foreach" loop executes a number of times equal to the items inside the collection. In the code block, we printed each character of the string "Welcome to C#" on a new line.

Output4:

```
W
e
l
c
o
m
e

t
o

C
#
```

Exercise 4

Task:

Using a "while" loop, display the sum of all the even numbers between 0 and 100 (inclusive).

Solution:

```
using System;
usingSystem.Diagnostics;

namespaceMyCSharpApplication
{
class Program
    {
static void Main(string[] args)
        {

inti = 0;
int sum = 0;
while (i<= 100)
            {
if (i % 2 == 0)
              {
sum = sum + i;
              }
i++;
          }
Console.WriteLine("Sum of even numbers between 0 and
100 is:"+sum);
Console.Read();
        }
    }
}
```

Chapter 5: Arrays

Suppose you have to store the salaries of three employees. You can declare three integer type variables which can store those salaries. What if you have to store the salaries of one hundred employees? Will you declare one hundred integer type variables and then individually store the salary of each employee in one variable? This is one solution. However, accessing variables this way is very cumbersome. Also, this approach results in verbose code. A better approach is to use C# arrays. An array contains a collection of items of a particular type. Arrays store data in contiguous memory locations which improves its efficiency. Each item in an array is called.

Contents:

- **Array Syntax**
- **One-dimensional Array**
- **Two-dimensional Array**

1- Array Syntax

An array has the following syntax:

```
type [] array-name = new type [size];
```

An array starts with the type of element it is going to store, followed by a square bracket and finally the name of the array. At this point in time, an array is only declared and no memory locations are reserved for it. To initialize an array, you use the "new" keyword followed by the type of the array. This is followed by square brackets, and, inside those square brackets, you specify the size of the array. The size specifies the number of elements an array can store. The following piece of code specifies how to initialize an integer type array named salaries with a size of 10.

```
int [] salaries = new int [10];
```

2- One-Dimensional Array

An array which stores elements in one direction, i.e. in the form of a column or row, is called a one-dimensional array. The "salaries" array which we declared in the last section was a one-dimensional array. A one-dimensional array is initialized using one square bracket after the array type. To see a one-dimensional array in action, have a look at the first example of this chapter.

Example1:

```
using System;

namespaceMyCSharpApplication
```

```
{
class Program
    {
static void Main(string[] args)
        {

int[] salaries = new int[10] { 78, 15, 27, 87, 56,
74, 12, 36, 98, 41 };


int a = salaries[0];
int b = salaries[5];

Console.WriteLine(a + b);

salaries[0] = 25;
salaries[5] = 25;


            a = salaries[0];
            b = salaries[5];

Console.WriteLine(a + b);

Console.Read();
        }
    }
}
```

In Example1, we initialized the array "salaries" and stored 10 elements in this array at initialization time. This is one way to store elements in the array. You initialize the array and, on the same line, you enter the elements inside the curly brackets that follow after the square brackets containing the size. Inside the curly bracket, you separate each element with a comma. An array has a zero based storage index. This means that the first element of the array is stored at 0th index while the last element is stored at n-1st index, where n is the size of the array. To access the element at any index, you use the name of the array followed by square brackets. Inside the square brackets, you mention the index. For instance, in Example1, the element at the 0th index of the salaries array is stored in integer variable "a", while the element at the 5th index is stored in variable "b". On the console, the sum of these two variables is printed. Then the array indexes zero and five are updated with value 25. On the console window, their sum is again printed, which now contains the updated value. The output of the code in Example1 is shown below.

Output1:

```
152
50
```

In Chapter 4, we studied the "foreach" loop, which can be used to iterate over any set or list of items. In addition to the "foreach" loop, the "for" loop can also be used to iterate over an array. In Example2, we shall see how an array can be iterated via "for" and "foreach" loops.

Example2:

```
using System;

namespaceMyCSharpApplication
{
class Program
    {
```

```
static void Main(string[] args)
        {

int[] salaries = new int[10] { 78, 15, 27, 87, 56,
74, 12, 36, 98, 41 };


for (inti = 0; i< 10; i++ )
            {
Console.Write(salaries[i] + " ");
            }

Console.WriteLine();

foreach (int n in salaries)
            {
Console.Write(n+" ");
            }

Console.Read();
        }
    }
}
```

In Example2, the "salaries" array has again been initialized with some random variables. We first iterated the array with a "for" loop, then we iterated over the "salaries" array using a "foreach" loop. The output of the code in Example2 is as follows.

Output2:

```
78 15 27 87 56 74 12 36 98 41
78 15 27 87 56 74 12 36 98 41
```

3- Two-dimensional Array

A one-dimensional array stores data in the form of a single column or row. A two-dimensional array, often referred as an array of arrays, stores data in the form of multiple rows and columns. Data is stored in the memory in the form of a matrix. To initialize a two-dimensional array, you simply have to put a comma inside the square bracket that follows after the type of the array. On the left side, after the new keyword and inside the square brackets, you have to mention the number of rows and columns that the array will contain. Rows and columns should be separated by commas. Look at Example3 to see two-dimensional arrays in action.

Example3:

```
using System;

namespaceMyCSharpApplication
{
class Program
    {
static void Main(string[] args)
        {

int[,] salaries = new int [2,3];

salaries[0,0] = 10; // First row first column
salaries[0,1] = 20; // First row second column
salaries[0, 2] = 30; // First row third column

salaries[1, 0] = 40; // 2nd row first column
salaries[1, 1] = 50; // 2nd row second column
```

```
salaries[1, 2] = 60; // 2nd row third column

for (inti = 0; i< 2; i++)
            {
for (int j = 0; j < 3; j++)
                {
Console.Write(salaries[i, j]+"   ");
                }
Console.WriteLine();
            }
Console.Read();
        }
    }
}
```

In Example1, we initialized a two-dimensional array, "salaries", with two rows and three columns. We then accessed each index and stored some random integer values. To access a particular index of a two-dimensional array, you write the name of the array followed by the square bracket. Inside the square brackets, you first enter the row number, then comma, and then the column number. To iterate over a two-dimensional array requires nested "for" loops where the outer loop iterates over each row and the inner loop iterates over each column. This is demonstrated in Example3. The output of the code in Example3 is as follows.

Output3:

```
10   20   30
40   50   60
```

Exercise 5

Task:

Using nested "for" loops, store the table of 2,3,4, and 5 in a two-dimensional array and then display the elements of the array on screen.

Solution

```
using System;

namespaceMyCSharpApplication
{
class Program
    {
static void Main(string[] args)
        {

int[,] tables = new int [4,10];

for (inti = 2; i< 6; i++)
            {
for (int j = 0; j <10; j++)
                {
tables[i-2,j] = i*(j+1);


                }
            }

for (inti = 0; i< 4; i++)
            {
for (int j = 0; j < 10; j++)
```

```
                {
Console.Write(tables[i, j]+"  ");
                }
Console.WriteLine();
            }
Console.Read();
        }
    }
}
```

Chapter 6: Objects and Classes

In the first five chapters, we covered most of the basic C# programming concepts. From this chapter onwards, we are going to study some of the advanced programming concepts, starting with object oriented programming. In object oriented programming (OOP), all the software components are viewed in the context of real world objects. For instance, you are developing some car racing game; you will identify the objects in the real world car racing. A driver can be an object, a car can be another object, and steering is also an object. When you develop your game you will create these objects in your program. These objects will interact with each other, resulting in fully functional racing car game. This is just a crude example of how modules are developed in OOP programming. OOP offers advantages such as code modularity, usability, and maintainability.

Contents

1- Objects and Classes

Anything which has some properties and can perform some functions is worthy of being implemented as an object in an OOP. As aforementioned, a player in a racing car game can be considered an object since it contains properties like a name, age, country, etc. A player can also perform functions like starting the car, increasing the speed, turning left, turning right, etc. A player is a perfect candidate for being implemented as an object.

Before diving into the code, an important distinction needs to be made here between a class and an object. A class is similar to a blue print. It has no physical existence in the memory. Class depicts how the object looks. Multiple objects can be created from one class. An object, on the other hand, has an actual physical existence in the memory. A class is like a blueprint while an object is the house built according to that blueprint.

To see how objects are created, have a look at the first example of this chapter.

Example1:

Add a new class to your project and name it "Player". The contents of the player class should be exactly like the following code snippet.

```
class Player
    {
string name;
int age;
string country;
    }
```

This is the structure of the player class. From this structure, it can be assumed that the object of the class will contain three variables: name, age, and country. The memory occupied by the object of the player will be roughly equal to the sum of the memories occupied by the variables name, age, and country. The "Player" class would have been created in the same namespace in which your "Program" class resides.

Open the "Program" class code and make following changes.

```
using System;

namespaceMyCSharpApplication
{
class Program
    {
static void Main(string[] args)
        {
            Player p = new Player();
            p.name = "Alan";
p.age = 25;
p.country = "USA";

Console.WriteLine(p.name +","+p.age+","+p.country);

Console.Read();
        }
    }
}
```

In the Program.cs file above, we created an object "p" in the "Player" class. To create an object of any class, use the "new" keyword followed by the constructor of the class. We will dig deeper into constructors in the next section. For now, assume that "Player()" is the default constructor of the "Player" class. Calling "new" followed by the constructor of any class creates an object of that class in memory and returns its reference. This reference can be stored in the variable of that class. In Example1, we created a variable "p" in class "Player". This variable "p" stores the reference of the object in the "Player" class. To access the members of an object, use the reference variable then a dot (.) followed by the property that you want to access. For instance, if you want to access the name of the object "p", you will use p.name. In this way, we stored three random values in name, age, and country. Finally, we print these values on the output console.

Output1:

```
Alan,25,USA
```

2- Constructor

A constructor is a function which creates an object of a class and returns its reference to the calling function. The name of the constructor is exactly the same as the name of the class in which it is written. A constructor has no return type, not even void. A constructor can also be used to initialize the member variables of the class when the object is being created. In the second example of this chapter, we will see how a constructor can be used to initialize member variables.

Example2:

Make the following changes in the "Player" class you created in Example1.

```
using System;

namespaceMyCSharpApplication
{
class Player
    {
public string name;
publicint age;
public string country;

public Player()
        {
name = "Scott";
age = 30;
country = "UK";


        }
    }
}
```

In the above code, we created a constructor which initializes the variables name, age, and country. Name becomes "Scott", age becomes "30", and country becomes "UK". When the object of this class is created calling this constructor, these three variables will automatically be initialized and will be readily available for printing on screen. To see their values on the console, make the following changes in the "Program" class.

```
using System;

namespaceMyCSharpApplication
```

```
{
class Program
    {
static void Main(string[] args)
        {
            Player p = new Player();


Console.WriteLine(p.name +","+p.age+","+p.country);
Console.Read();
        }
    }
}
```

The output of the code in Example2 is as follows:

Output2:

```
Scott,30,UK
```

- **Parameterized Constructor**

You can also initialize the member variables of the class using a constructor by passing arguments to the constructor while creating the object of the class. The constructor, which takes parameter from the calling function, is called a parameterized constructor. Example3 demonstrates usage of the parameterized constructor in C#.

Example3:

Make the following changes in the Player class:

```
using System;

namespaceMyCSharpApplication
{
class Player
    {
public string name;
publicint age;
public string country;

public Player(string name, int age, string country)
        {
            this.name = name;
this.age = age;
this.country = country;


        }
    }
}
```

In the above code snippet, we have entered three variables in the round brackets after the constructor name. These are the parameters, which are separated by commas. To call this constructor, we have to pass three parameters in the call to constructor. These parameters should match the parameter type in the constructor declaration. Also, the order of the passed parameters should match the order of the parameters in the constructor declaration. For instance, in the call to this parameterized constructor, the first parameter should be string, the second should be integer, and the third should be again string. Make the following changes in the "Program" class to see how this works.

```
using System;

namespaceMyCSharpApplication
{
class Program
    {
static void Main(string[] args)
        {
            Player p = new Player("Joseph", 35,
"Italy");


Console.WriteLine(p.name +", "+p.age+", "+p.country);
Console.Read();
        }
    }
}
```

The output of the code in Example3 is as follows:

Output3:

```
Joseph,35,Italy
```

- **Overloaded Constructor**

You can have two or more parameterized constructors in your class. When the object of the class is created, the constructor whose parameters match with the parameter in the call to the constructor would be called. This concept sounds confusing at first. The fourth example of this chapter demonstrates the concept of an overloaded constructor.

Example4:

Make the following changes in the "Player" class.

Player.cs

```
using System;


namespaceMyCSharpApplication
{
class Player
    {
public string name;
publicint age;
public string country;

public Player(string name, int age, string country)
        {
            this.name = name;
this.age = age;
this.country = country;


        }

public Player(string name)
        {
            this.name = name;
        }
    }
}
```

In the "Player" class, you can see that now there are two
parameterized constructors. The first constructor is similar to the
one in Example3 and it takes three parameters. The second
constructor takes one parameter. The constructor that is called

when an object is created depends on the call to the constructor. If the call contains one string type parameter, the second constructor will be called. However, if the call contains three parameters(string, int, string), the first constructor would be called.

Make the following changes in the "Program" class to see difference between the calls to the two constructors in the "Player" class.

Program.cs

```
using System;

namespaceMyCSharpApplication
{
class Program
    {
static void Main(string[] args)
        {
            Player   p   =   new   Player("Joseph",   35,
"Italy");

            Player p2 = new Player("Susan");
            p2.age = 40;
            p2.country = "France";

        Console.WriteLine(p.name + "," + p.age + "," +
p.country);
Console.WriteLine(p2.name
+","+p2.age+","+p2.country);



Console.Read();
```

```
        }
    }
}
```

The output of the code in Example4 is as follows:

Output4:

```
Joseph,35,Italy
Susan,40,France
```

Exercise 6

Task:

Create a class named "Product" with three properties: name, price, and category. Add a parameterized constructor which initializes these three properties. Add another constructor which initializes the first two properties. In the "Program" class, create two objects of "Product" class by calling the two overloaded constructors of the "Player" class. Display the properties of both objects on the console.

Solution:

Product Class:

```
using System;
```

```csharp
usingSystem.Collections.Generic;
usingSystem.Linq;
usingSystem.Text;
usingSystem.Threading.Tasks;

namespaceMyCSharpApplication
{
class Product
    {
public string name;
publicint price;
public string category;

public   Product(string   name,   int   price,   string
category)
        {
            this.name = name;
this.price = price;
this.category = category;
        }

public Product(string name, int price)
        {
            this.name = name;
this.price = price;
        }

    }
}
```

Program Class

```
using System;

namespaceMyCSharpApplication
{
class Program
    {
static void Main(string[] args)
        {
            Product  p  =  new  Product("Laptop",  40,
"Electronics");

            Product p2 = new Product("Apple", 2);
            p2.category = "Fruits";


Console.WriteLine(p2.name
+","+p2.price+","+p2.category);

Console.WriteLine(p.name  + ","  +  p.price  +  ","  +
p.category);

Console.Read();
        }
    }
}
```

Chapter 7: Access Modifiers and Methods

In the last chapter, we studied what objects and classes are and how the member variables of a class can be initialized via constructor. We also studied different types of constructors. In this chapter, we are going to study how objects act to perform certain functionalities. In object oriented programming (OOP), this is achieved via methods. However, before diving into the details of methods, we shall study another important concept: access modifiers in C#.

Contents

- **Access Modifiers**
- **Methods in C#**

1- Access Modifiers

From the beginning of this book, we have been using the keyword "public" with variables. This is one of the five access modifiers available in C#. Access modifiers control access to a particular variable. For instance, a member variable marked "public" can be accessed anywhere. However, a variable marked "private" is accessible only within the class in which it exists. Table 1.0 contains C#'s five access modifiers along with their functionalities.

Access Modifier	Functionality
public	Accessible everywhere
internal	Accessible only to the classes within the assembly and friend assemblies
protected	Accessible only within the class and its derived classes
private	Accessible only within the class
Protected-internal	Accessible where protected or internal are accessible

2- Methods

As aforementioned, C# classes and objects act via methods. To understand the concept of methods in C#, let's jump straight to the first example of this chapter.

Example1:

Add a new class named "Product" to the existing project. The contents of the "Product" class should be similar to the following code snippet.

<u>Product.cs</u>

```
using System;


namespaceMyCSharpApplication
{
class Product
    {
        public string name;
public   int price;
public string category;

public   Product(string   name,   int   price,   string
category)
        {
            this.name = name;
this.price = price;
this.category = category;
        }

public void IncreasePrice()
        {
price += 10;
        }


    }
}
```

The produce class contains three member variables: name, price, and category. The class contains a constructor which initializes these three variables. After the constructor, we have added a method named "IncreasePrice". The syntax of a method is simple; it starts with an access modifier, which is public in this case. After that, the return type of the method is mentioned. A return type is the type of the value returned by the method. Since our "IncreasePrice" method doesn't return any value, we specified its return type as void. After the return type, the name of the method is written (in our case, this is "IncreasePrice"). The opening and closing round brackets contain parameters. Since we don't want our "IncreasePrice" method to accept any parameter, we left the brackets empty. Notice that the method declaration is quite similar to the constructor declaration. A constructor is, in fact, a method with no return type. A method is called using the object of the class by the appending dot operator followed by the method name after the object of the class. Modify the "Program" class so that it looks like the one in following code snippet.

Program.cs

```
using System;

namespaceMyCSharpApplication
{
class Program
    {
static void Main(string[] args)
        {
            Product   p   =   new   Product("Grapes",   40,
"Food");

Console.WriteLine("The   price   of   product   "+p.name+   "
is: "+p.price);
```

```
p.IncreasePrice();

Console.WriteLine("The   new   price   of   product   "   +
p.name + " is: " + p.price);

Console.Read();
        }
    }
}
```

In the "Program", we created the object of "Product" class using a parameterized constructor. The initial value of the variable "price" is set to 40. We displayed this price on the console. Then we called the "IncreasePrice" method on the object "p" of the "Product" class. The value of the "price" variable is incremented by 10 every time the "IncreasePrice" method is called. Since we called this method only once, the price is incremented by 10 only once; the new price would be 40+10 = 50. We then printed this new price on the console just to make sure the price was incremented. The output of the code in Example1 is as follows:

Output1:

```
The price of product Grapes is: 40
The new price of product Grapes is: 50
```

- **Passing Parameters to a Method**

Just like we have parameterized constructors, we also have parameterized methods. For instance, instead of increasing the

64

price of the price variable by 10 every time, we can also pass a value of our choice. Types of parameters which a method can accept are mentioned in the round brackets that follow the method name. In the second example, we will see how we can increase the price by the value of our choice by passing the value as a parameter to the "IncreasePrice" method.

Example2:

Change the code in the "Product" and "Program" classes as follows:

Product.cs

```
using System;

namespaceMyCSharpApplication
{
class Product
    {
public string name;
public  int price;
public string category;

public   Product(string   name,   int   price,   string
category)
        {
            this.name = name;
this.price = price;
this.category = category;
        }

public void IncreasePrice(int price)
        {
this.price += price;
        }
```

65

```
        }
}
```

```
using System;

namespaceMyCSharpApplication
{
class Program
    {
static void Main(string[] args)
        {
             Product  p  =  new  Product("Grapes",  40,
"Food");

Console.WriteLine("The  price  of  product  "+p.name+  "
is: "+p.price);

p.IncreasePrice(25);

Console.WriteLine("The  new  price  of  product  "  +
p.name + " is: " + p.price);

Console.Read();
        }
    }
}
```

Output2:

```
The price of product Grapes is: 40
```

66

```
The new price of product Grapes is: 65
```

• Returning Values From Method

In both of our first two examples, the method "IncreasePrice" did not return any value. The return type of the method was void. However, we can also force a method to return a value by changing its return type. For instance, we can retrieve the increased price from the "IncreasePrice" method by changing its return type to "int" and then using "return" at the end of the method, followed by the value to be returned. This is explained in the following example.

Example3:

Change the code in the "Product" and "Program" classes as follows:

Product.cs

```
using System;

namespaceMyCSharpApplication
{
class Product
    {
public string name;
public  int price;
public string category;

public   Product(string   name,   int   price,   string
category)
        {
            this.name = name;
```

```
this.price = price;
this.category = category;
        }


publicintIncreasePrice(int price)
        {
this.price += price;

returnthis.price;
        }
    }
}
```

Program.cs

```
using System;

namespaceMyCSharpApplication
{
class Program
    {
static void Main(string[] args)
        {
            Product p = new Product("Grapes", 40,
"Food");

Console.WriteLine("The price of product "+p.name+
"is: "+p.price);

Console.WriteLine("The new price of product " +
p.name + "is: " + p.IncreasePrice(20));

Console.Read();
        }
```

```
        }
}
```

```
The price of product Grapesis: 40
The new price of product Grapesis: 60
```

Exercise 7

Task:

Create a class named "Car". Create two variables named "name" and "speed" inside the class. Initialize these variables using a parameterized constructor. Create a method inside the "Car" class. This method should accept an integer value and decrease the speed of the car by that value. The method should return the decreased speed to the calling function. In the "Program" class, display the decreased speed on console.

Solution:

Car Class:

```
using System;
usingSystem.Collections.Generic;


namespaceMyCSharpApplication
{
class Car
    {
public string name;
publicint speed;

public Car(string name, int speed)
        {
            this.name = name;
this.speed = speed;
        }

publicintDecreaseSpeed(int speed)
        {
this.speed -= speed;
returnthis.speed;
        }
    }
}
```

Program Class:

```
using System;
usingSystem.Diagnostics;


namespaceMyCSharpApplication
{
class Program
    {
static void Main(string[] args)
        {
            Car c = new Car("Ford", 105);

Console.WriteLine("Initial    Speed    of    car    is
"+c.speed);

Console.WriteLine("Decreased  Speed  of  car  is    "  +
c.DecreaseSpeed(15));

Console.Read();
        }
    }
}
```

Chapter 8: Inheritance & Polymorphism

In the last two chapters, we covered basic object oriented concepts (OOP). In this chapter, we are going to study two advanced OOPs: Inheritance and Polymorphism. Like all the other OOP concepts, inheritance in OOP is similar to the concept of real world inheritance. A child inherits some of the traits of his/her parents while also having some traits specific to him/her. In object oriented programming, the concept is similar. Inheritance also exists between different classes and is marked by an Is-A relationship. For instance, a "laptop" is a product, a "car" is a vehicle, and an "employee" is a person. Here, "laptop" is a child class of product, "car" is child of vehicle, and "employee" is a child class of person. The concept of polymorphism is based on inheritance; we will study that in a later section.

Contents

- **Inheritance**

- **Polymorphism**

1- Inheritance

The idea of inheritance is that all the traits that are common between the child classes are implemented in the parent class, while traits that are specific to individual child classes are implemented in the respective child classes. For instance, take a parent product class and its child software and hardware product. Both software and hardware products have a name and price. Therefore, we can include both name and price properties in the parent product class. Classes that inherit the parent class have all the attributes of the parent class by default. However, software has no weight while hardware product has some weight. This means that the attribute weight is unique to hardware class; therefore, it cannot be implemented in the parent class. Similarly, we assume that software has a version number while hardware has no version number. Here, version is unique to the software class and cannot be implemented in the parent class. This scenario has been implemented in Example1.

Example1:

Add three classes(Product, Hardware, and Software) to your project. The code markup of these three classes should be as follows:

Product.cs

```
using System;


namespaceMyCSharpApplication
```

```
{
class Product
    {
public string name;
public  int price;


    }
}
```

In the Product class, we added only two attributes: name and price.

Software.cs

```
using System;

namespaceMyCSharpApplication
{
class Software : Product
    {
publicint version;

public Software(string name, int price, int version)
        {
            this.name = name;
this.price = price;
this.version = version;
        }
    }
}
```

Have a look at the declaration of the software class. After the name of the class, we appended a semicolon followed by

"Product". This is how the child class inherits the parent class. You have to append a semicolon after the child class name followed by the class name which you want your child class to inherit. In the above code, the "Software" class is inheriting the "Product" class. In the software classes, we added only one attribute named "version". Then we added a parameterized constructor with three parameters. Inside the constructor, we initialized name, price, and version attributes. Notice that the "Software" class doesn't contain name and price attributes, but since it is inheriting the "Product" class, which contains these attributes, the child "Software" class has these attributes by default. In the same way, we inherited the "Hardware" class from the "Product" class and initialized its attributes.

Hardware.cs

```
using System;

namespaceMyCSharpApplication
{
class Hardware : Product
    {
publicint weight;

public Hardware(string name, int price, int weight)
        {
            this.name = name;
this.price = price;
this.weight = weight;


        }


    }
}
```

In the "Program" class, we create objects of both the "Software" and "Hardware" classes using their parameterized constructors and then display the names of both of the objects.

Program.cs

```
using System;

namespaceMyCSharpApplication
{
class Program
    {
static void Main(string[] args)
        {

            Software  s  =  new  Software("windows  7",
150, 3);
            Hardware  h  =  new  Hardware("Laptop",  500,
2);

Console.WriteLine("You bought:  " + s.name + " and " +
h.name);

Console.Read();
        }
    }
}
```

Output1:

```
You bought: windows 7 and Laptop
```

2- Polymorphism

The object of the parent class can hold objects of child classes. The parent class acts differently depending on the reference of the object it is storing. This concept lies in the basis of polymorphism. Suppose the "Product" class has a method, "DisplayProduct", which displays the name of the product on screen. Both the child classes also have a method called "DisplayProduct". The method inside the "Software" class displaysname and version while the method inside the "Hardware" class displays name and price. Since the object of the "Product" class can store references of the "Product", "Software", and "Hardware" classes, the question arises here that if "DisplayProduct" method is called on the object, which method will be called? Will it be of "Product", "Software", or "Hardware" class? The answer is the "DisplayProduct" method will call the class whose reference is stored in the object of the "Product" class. This concept has been explained in Example2.

Example2

Make the following modification to the "Product", "Software", and "Hardware" classes added in Example1.

Product.cs

```
using System;

namespaceMyCSharpApplication
{
class Product
    {
public string name;
public  int price;
```

```
public virtual void DisplayProduct()
        {
Console.WriteLine("This is a parent class: " + name);
        }


    }
}
```

If child classes have to contain a method with the same name as in the parent class, that method has to be marked virtual in the parent class. This is why we marked the "DisplayProduct" method virtual in the parent class. When this method is added in the child class, it has to be marked with the keyword "override". This is shown in both the "Software" and "Hardware" classes.

Software.cs

```
using System;

namespaceMyCSharpApplication
{
class Software : Product
    {
publicint version;

public Software(string name, int price, int version)
        {
            this.name = name;
this.price = price;
this.version = version;
        }

public override void DisplayProduct()
```

```
        {
Console.WriteLine("You bought  " + name + ", version
"+ version);
        }
    }
}
```

Hardware.cs

```
using System;

namespaceMyCSharpApplication
{
class Hardware : Product
    {
publicint weight;

public Hardware(string name, int price, int weight)
        {
            this.name = name;
this.price = price;
this.weight = weight;

        }

public override void DisplayProduct()
        {
Console.WriteLine("You bought " + name + ", weight "
+ weight);
        }

    }
}
```

In the "Program" class, we created the object of parent "Product" class and then stored references of the objects of the "Product", "Software", and "Hardware" classes in it. Then we called the "DisplayProduct" method sequentially. You will see that, in the output, different "DisplayProduct" methods will be called depending on the references stored in the "Product" class object.

Program.cs

```
using System;

namespaceMyCSharpApplication
{
class Program
    {
static void Main(string[] args)
        {

            Product p = new Product();
            p.name = "Apple";
p.price = 10;
p.DisplayProduct();

            p = new Software("windows 7", 150, 3);
p.DisplayProduct();

            p = new Hardware("Laptop", 500, 2);
p.DisplayProduct();

Console.Read();
        }
    }
}
```

Output2:

```
This is a parent class: Apple
You bought windows 7, version 3
You bought Laptop, weight 2
```

Exercise 8

Task:

Create a class named "Shape". Add one member variable, "name", to this class. Add a method called "DisplayName" which displays the variable name on console screen with the appropriate statement. Create two classes, "Triangle" and "Pentagon". Create parameterized constructors which initialize variable names in both the "Triangle" and "Pentagon" classes. These classes will implement their own "DisplayName" method. Using a test class, such as Program.cs, show how polymorphism can be achieved in this scenario.

Solution:

Shape Class:

```csharp
using System;

namespaceMyCSharpApplication
{
class Shape
    {
public string name;

public virtual void DisplayName()
        {
            Console.WriteLine("This    is    a    parent
class named: " + name);
        }
    }
}
```

Triangle Class

```csharp
using System;

namespaceMyCSharpApplication
{
class Triangle: Shape
    {

public Triangle (string name)
        {
            this.name = name;
        }

        public override void DisplayName()
```

```
            {
                Console.WriteLine  ("This   is   a   child
class named: " + name);
            }


        }
}
```

Pentagon Class

```
using System;


namespaceMyCSharpApplication
{
class Pentagon: Shape
    {
public Pentagon (string name)
            {
                    this.name = name;
            }

        public override void DisplayName()
            {
                Console.WriteLine  ("This   is   a   child
class named: " + name);
            }
        }
}

    }
```

Program Class

```csharp
using System;

namespaceMyCSharpApplication
{
class Program
    {
static void Main(string[] args)
        {

            Shape s = new Shape();
            s.name = "Shape";
s.DisplayName();

            s = new Triangle("Triangle");
s.DisplayName();

            s = new Pentagon("Pentagon");
s.DisplayName();

Console.Read();
        }
    }
}
```

Chapter 9: Events and Delegates

In this chapter, we are going to study two very important concepts in C#: Delegates and Events. C#'s entire event handling mechanism is based on these two concepts. Delegates in C# are function pointers. They hold reference to a function. They provide decoupling between the calling function and the function being called. An event in C# is also a type of delegate. Events are used to invoke methods. For instance, when you click a button, an event fires which invokes all the methods associated with the event. In this chapter, we shall see these concepts in action.

Contents

- **Delegates**
- **Events**

1- Delegates

Delegates are classes which invoke a method which is passed to its constructor. Delegates store references to the method which is passed to it as a delegate. The first example of this chapter demonstrates how a delegate is created and how it is used to reference a method.

Example1:

```
using System;

namespaceMyCSharpApplication
{

public delegate intChangeIt(intnum);

class Program
    {
static void Main(string[] args)
        {

ChangeIt c = square;
Console.WriteLine("The square of 4 is: "+ c(4));

Console.Read();
        }

public static int square(intnum)
        {
returnnum * num;
        }
    }
}
```

In Example1, we created a delegate, "ChangeIt", by using the keyword "delegate". A delegate can only store references to methods that exactly match the signature of the delegate. For instance, in Example 1, the delegate signature is "intChangeit (intnum)". This means that this delegate can call any method which accepts an integer type variable as a parameter and returns an integer type variable. In the "Program" class, we created a static method called "square". The signature of this method matches the signature of the "ChangeIt" delegate. Inside the "Main" method, we create a variable, "c", of the delegate "ChangeIt" and assign it the method "square". To invoke the method, we simply pass the parameter to variable "c". For instance, if we pass 4 to variable "c", the value returned would be 16 because, internally, "c" would call the "square" method. We then display the returned value on the screen.

Output1:

```
The square of 4 is: 16
```

2- Events

Events are also a type of delegate; however, during declaration, the keyword "event" is appended before the delegate name. Like delegates, events are also hooked to methods. Events can execute methods with a signature similar to the signature of the delegate type of the event. When the event is fired, one or more methods can be executed. Example2 demonstrates how events are hooked to methods and how these methods are called when an event is fired.

Example2:

```
using System;

namespaceMyCSharpApplication
{
```

```
public delegate void DisplayNameHandler();


class Program
    {
public static event DisplayNameHandlerNameChanged;
static void Main(string[] args)
        {

NameChanged += DisplayFruit;
NameChanged += DisplayAnimal;
NameChanged += DisplayFlower;
NameChanged += DisplayColor;

NameChanged.Invoke();

Console.Read();
        }

public static void DisplayFruit()
        {
Console.WriteLine("This is an apple.");
        }

public static void DisplayAnimal()
        {
Console.WriteLine("This is a lion.");
        }

public static void DisplayFlower()
        {
Console.WriteLine("This is a rose.");
        }

public static void DisplayColor()
```

```
        {
Console.WriteLine("This is red.");
        }
    }
}
```

In Example 2, we created a delegate named "DisplayNameHandler". Inside the "Program" class, we created an event "NameChanged" of the delegate type "DisplayNameHandler". We declared four methods: "DisplayFruit", "DisplayAnimal", "DisplayFlower", and "DisplayColor". The signature of these methods is similar to the "DisplayNameHandler"; therefore, we can hook these four methods to the "NameChanged" event. To hook a method with any event, we simply add that method to the event name. In Example 1, the statement "NameChanged += DisplayFruit" depicts the hooking of method "DisplayFruit" to the "NameChanged" event. To fire an event, we simply call the "Invoke" method on that event. "Invoke" executes all the methods hooked with the "NameChanged" event in the order in which they are hooked. The output of the code in Example2 is as follows.

Output2:

```
This is an apple.
This is a lion.
This is a rose.
This is red.
```

Exercise 9

Task:

Create a delegate named "Calculations" which accepts two integer type parameters and returns one integer type value. In the "Program" class, create two methods, "sum" and "subtract", which have the same signature as the "Calculations" delegate. Create an object of the "Calculation" delegate and hook both the "sum" and "subtract" methods to it. Perform "sum" and "subtraction" on two random integers using the object of "Calculation" delegate hooked to the "sum" and "subtract" methods.

Solution

```
using System;

namespaceMyCSharpApplication
{

public delegate int Calculations(int num1, int num2);

class Program
    {

static void Main(string[] args)
        {

            Calculations c = Sum;

c(10, 5);

Console.WriteLine(c(10, 5));
```

```
            c += Subtract;
Console.WriteLine(c(10, 5));

Console.Read();
        }

public static int Sum(int num1, int num2)
        {
return num1 + num2;
        }

public static int Subtract (int num1, int num2)
        {
return num1 - num2;
        }

    }
}
```

Chapter 10: Multithreading

Up until this point, we have been working with single-threaded applications where program follow a single path of execution and only a single piece of code is executed at a particular time. This approach is suited to simple console based applications. However, in case of advanced GUI based applications, a single-threaded execution causes unresponsiveness and delayed execution. Consider a Windows form application where data has to be fetched before being displayed on the form. During the period when data is being fetched by the application, the user can do nothing on the front end of the form. If the database is huge, more time is spent fetching the data causing the front end of the application to behave unresponsively. Multithreading is the solution to such problems. In this chapter, we are going to study how to create threads and how they work together resulting in asynchronous program execution.

Contents

- **What is a thread?**

- **Thread Creation in C#**
- **Thread Join and Sleep**

1- What is a thread?

A thread is the smallest unit of execution. A thread runs inside a process. A process reserves operating system resources along with an exclusive execution environment. One process can have one or more threads. In single-threaded applications, only one thread runs inside a process, having exclusive access to all the process resources and the execution environment. In case of multithreaded applications, multiple threads run inside a process and they share several process resources, particularly memory and the execution environment. This sharing of resources leads to the solution of the unresponsiveness problem explained in the introduction. In multithreaded applications, one thread can fetch data from the database and store it in the shared memory, and the second thread can simultaneously display the fetched data on the front end of the application.

2- Thread Creation in C#

Creating a thread in C# is an extremely straight forward process. You just have to create an object of the "Thread". In the "Thread" class constructor, pass the method delegate that you want to run in a separate thread. Next, simply call the "Start" method on the object which you created. The first example of this chapter demonstrates thread creation and the execution process in detail. Have a look at it.

Example1:

```
using System;
usingSystem.Threading;

namespaceMyCSharpApplication
{
class Program
    {
static void Main(string[] args)
        {
            Thread t1 = new Thread(DisplayTwo);
            Thread t2 = new Thread(DisplayThree);

t1.Start();
t2.Start();

for (inti = 0; i< 100; i++)
            {
Console.Write("1");
            }
Console.Read();
        }

static void DisplayTwo()
        {
for (inti = 0; i< 100; i++)
            {
Console.Write("2");
            }
        }
static void DisplayThree()
        {
for (inti = 0; i< 100; i++)
            {
Console.Write("3");
            }
        }
```

```
        }
    }
}
```

To perform threading related tasks in your program, you need to import "System" and "System.Threading" namespace in your code. C# runtime creates one thread by default for every program. This is the thread in which the "Main" method runs. In Example2, inside the "Main" method, we have created two objects of "Thread" class. These objects have been named t1, and t2. In the constructor of the first object, t1, we passed the "DisplayTwo" method delegate. This method displays the digit "2" one hundred times on console. This method has been defined immediately after the "Main". Similarly, in the constructor of the t2 object, the "DisplayThree" method has been called. This method displays the digit "3" one hundred times on the screen. After initializing t1 and t2 inside the "Main" method, the "Start" method has been called on this object. Calling "Start" on the thread object creates a new path of execution which runs parallel to already-executing threads. At this point in time, three threads are running simultaneously: The main thread (which is running the "Main" method) and the t1 and t2 threads (which are running "DisplayTwo" and "DisplayThree" methods). This means that now we have three execution paths which are being executed simultaneously. These three paths are simultaneously trying to print the digits "1", "2", and "3" on the screen, one hundred times each. The output of the code in Example1 is as follows:

Output1

```
3212312313131321333322123121332231223322132231211121
2131313111121223331231231323232122321212332231123321
3312312232132231211323212231233221212111313212131233 2
2132133223122332133223131222233123322123313212331212 1
2311123212221313233211322312233213322123321232212213 3
31311313131131331333131111111111111
```

On the console screen, you will see that these digits are printed in a random order, although we called the "DisplayTwo" method first and then "DisplayThree". This is because all the threads are simultaneously trying to access the output console and print their respective digit; since control can only be accessed by one thread a time, it is randomly being allotted to each thread, resulting in a random display of digits on the output screen.

3- Thread Join and Sleep

In the previous section, we studied how multiple threads execute simultaneously. What if you want to let one thread complete its execution before proceeding further? To wait for an object to complete its execution, you call the "Join" method on that object. Similarly, if you want to stop thread execution for a particular time period, you can call the "Sleep" method on the thread class. This method takes times in milliseconds, or "TimeSpan" object, as its parameter.

To see this concept in action, have a look at the second example.

Example2:

```
using System;
usingSystem.Threading;
```

```
namespaceMyCSharpApplication
{
class Program
    {
static void Main(string[] args)
        {
            Thread t1 = new Thread(DisplayTwo);

t1.Start();

t1.Join();

Console.WriteLine("\n==================================
==========");
for (inti = 0; i< 100; i++)
            {
Console.Write("1");
if (i+1 == 50)
                {
Console.WriteLine("\nThread    Sleeps    here    for    5
seconds...");
Thread.Sleep(5000);
                }
            }
Console.Read();
        }

static void DisplayTwo()
        {
for (inti = 0; i< 100; i++)
            {
Console.Write("2");
            }
        }
    }
```

```
}
```

In Example2, we created thread object t1 which runs the "DisplayTwo" method. We start the thread execution by calling "Start" on this object. Immediately after calling "Start", we called "Join" on the t1 object in the next line. At this point, the thread inside which "Join" is called waits for the completion of the thread on which "Join" is called. This means that the "Main" method will wait for the complete execution of the t1 thread before executing itself further. After the t1 thread executes, the "Main" method will execute and the "for loop", which prints the digit "1", will also execute. When the "for loop" is executed 50 times, we call "Sleep" for 5 seconds. (5000 ms = 5 sec). The thread takes a break for 5 seconds and then prints the remaining digits. The output of the code in Example2 is as follows:

Output2:

```
2222222222222222222222222222222222222222222222222
2222222222222222222222222222222222222222222222
==============================================
11111111111111111111111111111111111111111111111111
Thread Sleeps here for 5 seconds...
11111111111111111111111111111111111111111111111111
```

Exercise 10

Task:

Create two threads inside the "Main" method. One thread should call a method which displays "+" on console one hundred times. The other method should display "X" on the screen one hundred times. The "Main" method should wait for the completion of both of these threads, and then it should display "#" on the screen 20 times. It should then wait for 3 seconds before displaying "#" again, this time 60 times. Finally, it should wait for 3 more seconds before displaying "#" 20 more times.

Solution

```
using System;
usingSystem.Threading;

namespaceMyCSharpApplication
{
class Program
    {
static void Main(string[] args)
        {
                Thread t1 = new Thread(DisplayPlus);
                Thread t2 = new Thread(DisplayMultiply);

t1.Start();
t2.Start();

t1.Join();
t2.Join();

Console.WriteLine("\n===================================
===========");
for (inti = 0; i< 100; i++)
            {
Console.Write("+");
if (i+1 == 20)
```

```
                    {
Console.WriteLine("\nThread    Sleeps    here    for    3
seconds...");
Thread.Sleep(3000);
                    }
if (i + 1 == 80)
                    {
Console.WriteLine("\nThread    Sleeps    here    for    3
seconds...");
Thread.Sleep(3000);
                    }


                }
Console.Read();
        }

static void DisplayPlus()
        {
for (inti = 0; i< 100; i++)
                {
Console.Write("+");
                }
        }

static void DisplayMultiply()
        {
for (inti = 0; i< 100; i++)
                {
Console.Write("X");
                }
        }
    }
}
```

Other Books by the Author

Java Programming

http://www.linuxtrainingacademy.com/java-programming

Java is one of the most widely used and powerful computer programming languages in existence today. Once you learn how to program in Java you can create software applications that run on servers, desktop computers, tablets, phones, Blu-ray players, and more.

Also, if you want to ensure your software behaves the same regardless of which operation system it runs on, then Java's "write once, run anywhere" philosophy is for you. Java was design to be platform independent allowing you to create applications that run on a variety of operating systems including Windows, Mac, Solaris, and Linux.

JavaScript: A Guide to Learning the JavaScript Programming Language

http://www.linuxtrainingacademy.com/javascript

JavaScript is a dynamic computer programming language that is commonly used in web browsers to control the behavior of web pages and interact with users. It allows for asynchronous communication and can update parts of a web page or even replace the entire content of a web page. You'll see JavaScript being used to display date and time information, perform animations on a web site, validate form input, suggest results as a user types into a search box, and more.

PHP

http://www.linuxtrainingacademy.com/php-book

PHP is one of the most widely used open source, server side programming languages. If you are interested in getting started with programming and want to get some basic knowledge of the language, then this book is for you! Popular websites such as Facebook and Yahoo are powered by PHP. It is, in a sense, the language of the web.

The book covers core PHP concepts, starting from the basics and moving into advanced object oriented PHP. It explains and demonstrates everything along the way. You'll be sure to be programming in PHP in no time.

Scrum Essentials: Agile Software Development and Agile Project Management for Project Managers, Scrum Masters, Product Owners, and Stakeholders
http://www.linuxtrainingacademy.com/scrum-book

You have a limited amount of time to create software, especially when you're given a deadline, self-imposed or not. You'll want to make sure that the software you build is at least decent but more importantly, on time. How do you balance quality with time? This book dives into these very important topics and more.

Made in the USA
Lexington, KY
25 August 2015